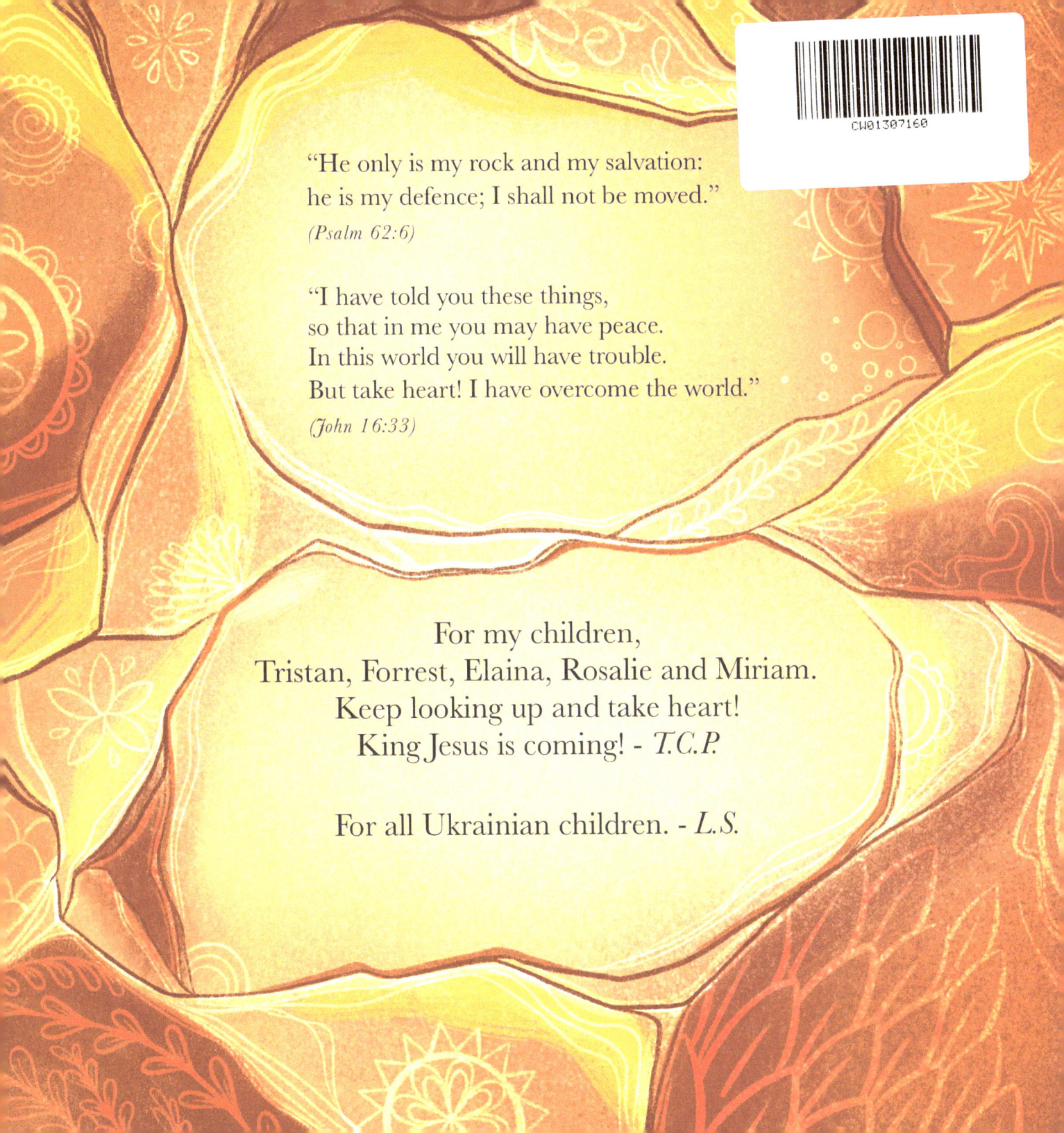

"He only is my rock and my salvation:
he is my defence; I shall not be moved."
(Psalm 62:6)

"I have told you these things,
so that in me you may have peace.
In this world you will have trouble.
But take heart! I have overcome the world."
(John 16:33)

For my children,
Tristan, Forrest, Elaina, Rosalie and Miriam.
Keep looking up and take heart!
King Jesus is coming! - *T.C.P.*

For all Ukrainian children. - *L.S.*

You can mock and persecute me,
you can cast me from the land,
but no matter where I go,
the Rock is where I stand.
Proverbs 26:24-26 / Matthew 5:10-12

7

8

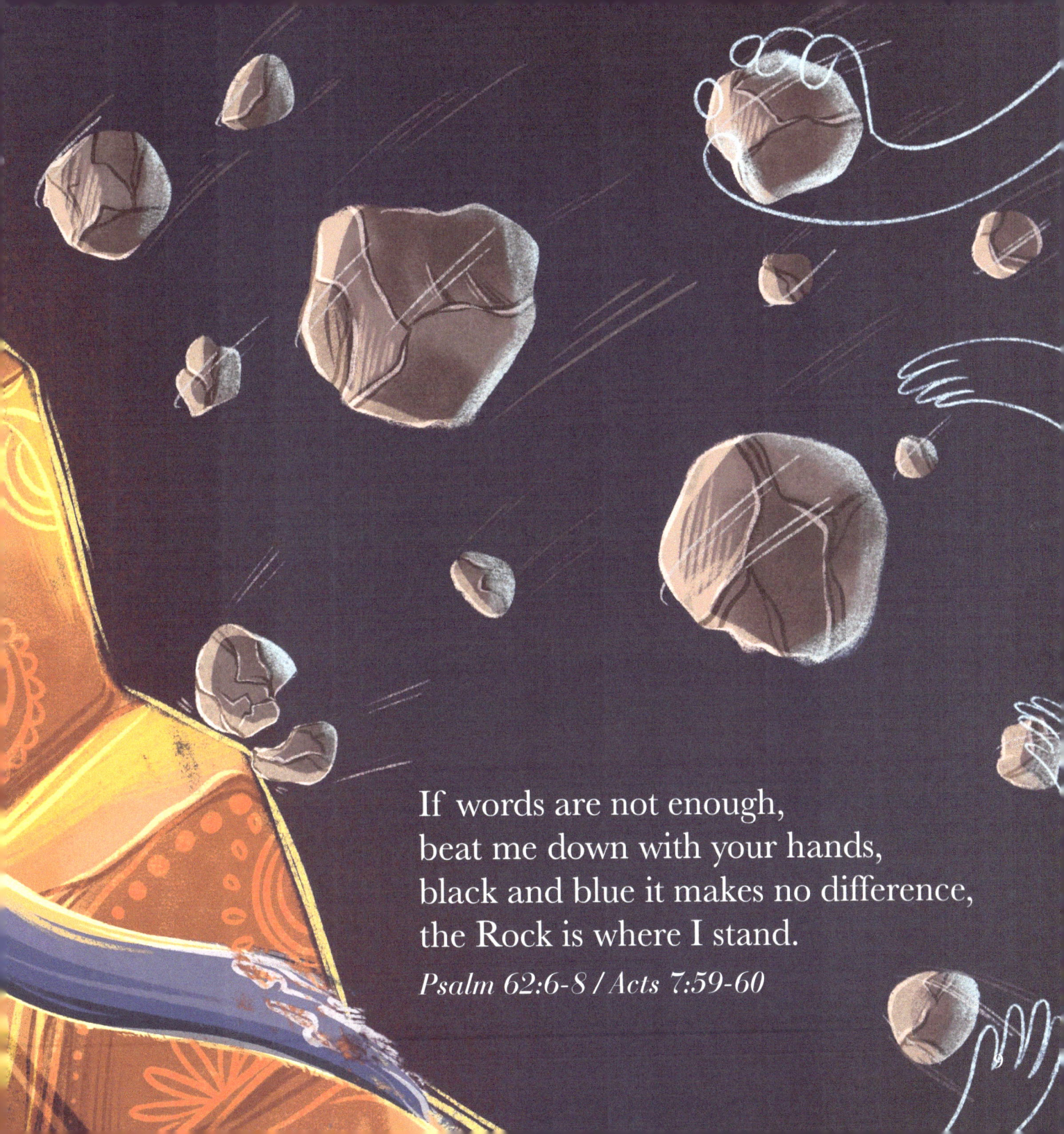

If words are not enough,
beat me down with your hands,
black and blue it makes no difference,
the Rock is where I stand.

Psalm 62:6-8 / Acts 7:59-60

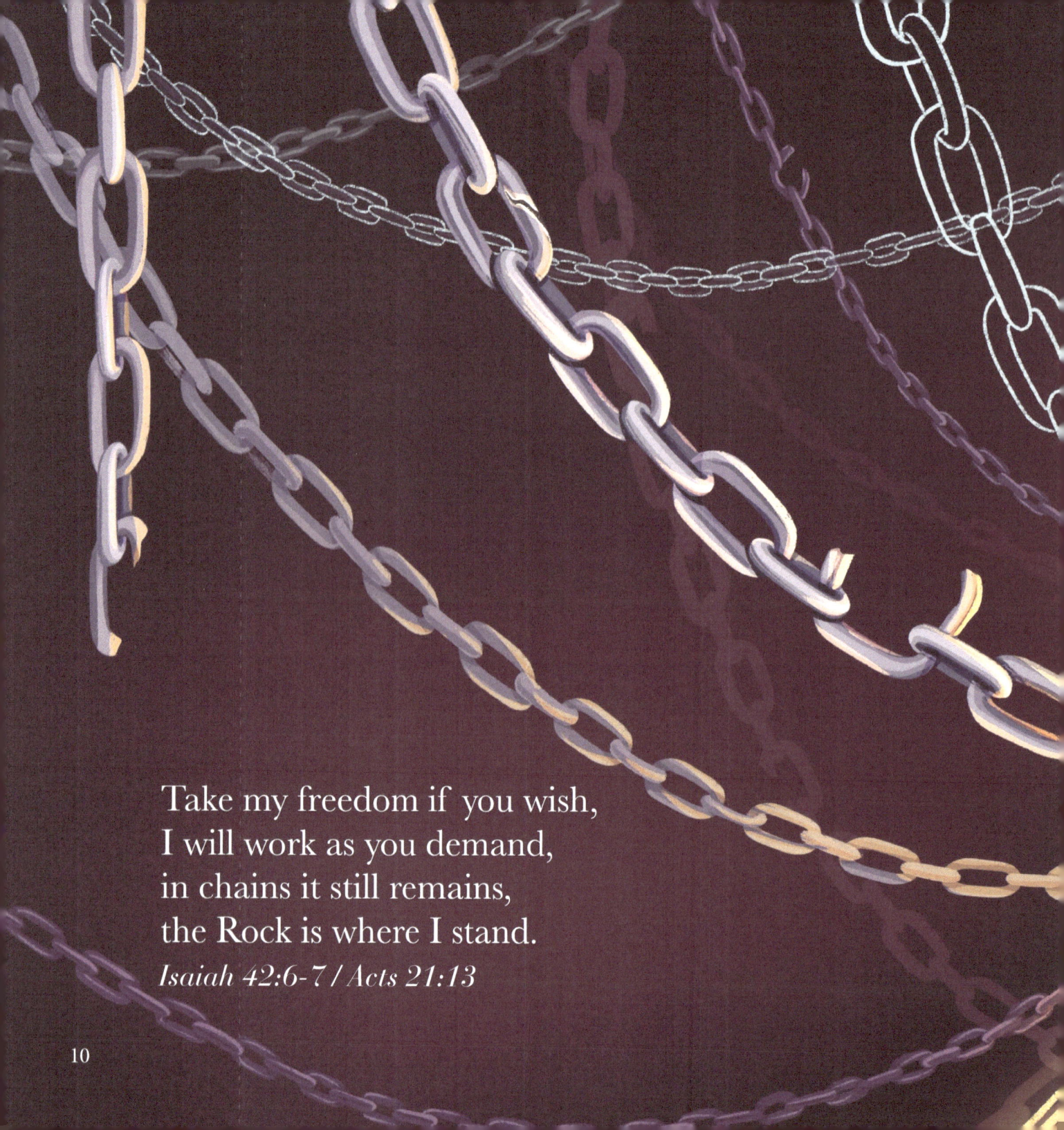

Take my freedom if you wish,
I will work as you demand,
in chains it still remains,
the Rock is where I stand.
Isaiah 42:6-7 / Acts 21:13

11

Even wage war upon me,
with the armies you command,
I will wait, sword in hand,
on the Rock where I stand.
1 Samuel 17:45-47 / Ephesians 6:10-18

13

As the world begins to crumble,
for they have built on sinking sand,
my faith and base remain,
for the Rock is where I stand.
Psalm 40:1-3 / Matthew 7:24-27

15

16

When Satan whispers lies,
to advance his wicked plan,
I find the truth in God's Word,
the solid Rock on which I stand.

Genesis 3:1 / John 1:1

18

As men like wolves surround me,
like a lost and lonely lamb,
my shepherd will protect me,
He is the Rock on which I stand.

Psalm 23:1-6 / John 10:11-18

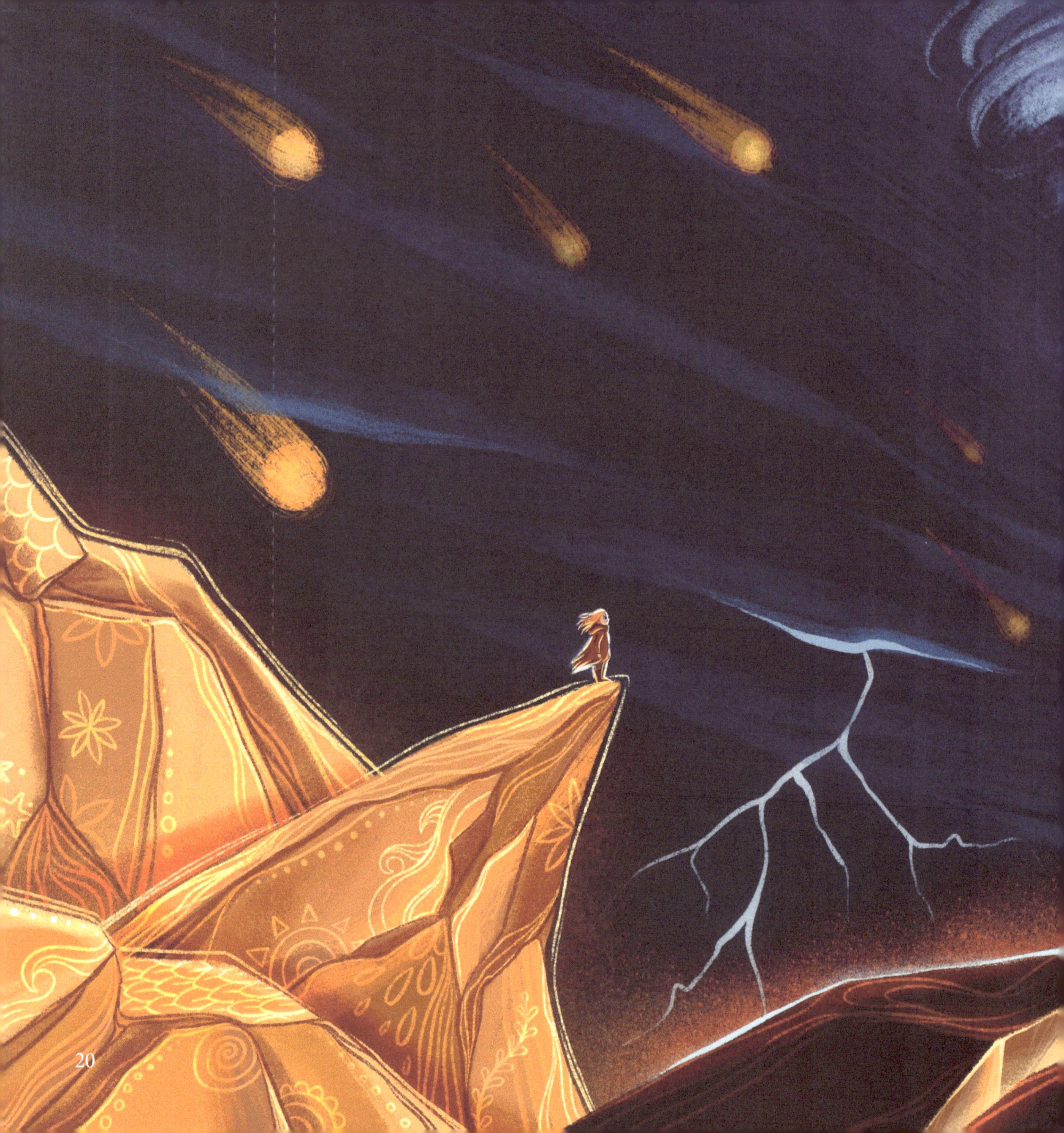

The Alpha and Omega,
He is the great I AM.
The King of all creation
and the Rock on which I stand.
Exodus 3:13-15 / Revelation 1:7-8

And when all seems truly lost and
I lay broken in defeat…

Psalm 57:4-5 / Romans 8:35-37

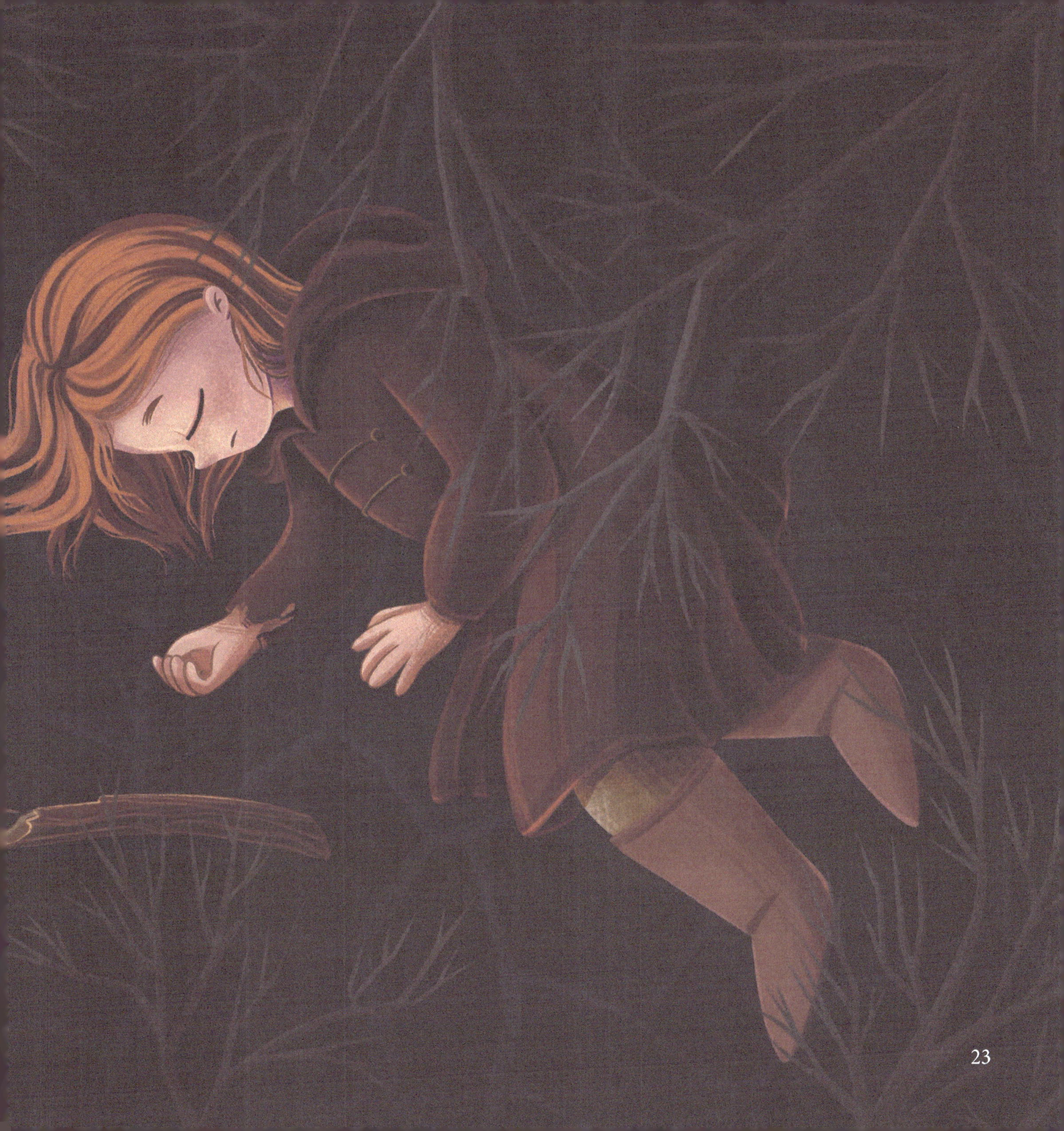

24

Jesus puts me on His back.
He is the Rock beneath my feet.

Ezekiel 34:11-16 / Revelation 21:1-7